The Bible Book
first produced in 1992
Group (TFG) – the Ch
of England High Scho

Revised and Updated 2025

Contents

Introduction	2
Learn for Yourself	4
Getting Started	7
Reading the Bible	
A Plan for Reading	
Finding the Right Translation	
Studying themes or characters	13
Studying verse by verse	15
How Long?	
Tools	17
Life Changing	18
Who wrote the Bible?	
Ways to Start	20
First Month Plan	23
Going Deeper	25
How to Pray	26

www.lumin.org.uk

Introduction

Imagine the scene: A rich father dies, leaving a will for his children but they ignore it, never bother to read it and never find out what it was they would inherit. A very unlikely story! But in many ways that is exactly how we react to the Bible. The Bible contains God's Will for US, and is packed with promises for us to inherit or accept as our own.

We arc fools if we ignore it, especially if we are Christians and are already members of God's Family; but in fairness we are also put off by what seems to be an impossible task: getting to know and understand ALL of the Bible takes a lifetime of devoted study .... so very often Christians just don't bother to start! Yet we read in the letter to Timothy (part of the New Testament) that *'All scripture is God-breathed and is useful for teaching [us], rebuking [us], correcting [us] and training [us] in righteousness, so that [we, the people of God] may be thoroughly equipped for every good work.'* 2 Timothy 3: 16,17 [*that means the Second Letter to Timothy, chapter 3 and verses 16 and 17*]. If scripture is so useful then we surely need to make a start at studying it.

First, however, we must be sure about what we believe about scripture. There are several possibilities, which one best fits what you think about the Bible right now?

The Bible is the Inspired Word of God and contains all we need for faith, and we can't get a true understanding of God's ways anywhere else (Reformed View)

As above, but we also need the traditions and teachings of the Church to get a full picture of how to come to God (Catholic View)

The Bible is just an ordinary, fallible book, which the Holy Spirit uses like any other to teach us (Liberal/Orthodox View)

Spend some time thinking about how you see the Bible ..... its important because you'll need to have an understanding of the nature of the Bible before it will really teach you anything. If the Bible is fallible (THREE) then you will want to question everything it says. On the other hand, if it is THE WORD of God (that is, as God wanted it and without error) then we cannot question its clear teaching. The only questions we can ask are about things that seem vague or uncertain, in order to clarify them.

This booklet is written assuming you hold positions ONE or TWO; that you accept the Bible to be authoritative and from God; that He wrote it to guide us and teach us and that it is relevant to us today. As we read it from this point of view we don't need to start pulling it to pieces with literary criticism about 'who wrote this bit' or 'this was added later'. The Bible was written as God wanted it and, provided we have a reliable translation, is exactly what He wants to say to us (whoever penned each section). So we need to read it, obey it and enjoy it. (See Appendices for advice on how to approach the accounts of Adam & Eve, Creation & Science, etc).

The aim of what follows is to help you to get into the Bible and start to learn for yourself what God is saying. So we approach it as a book written with authority by the One who created the Universe and who then came to earth to redeem us from our sins and restore us to fellowship with Himself. We read it as God's Will to us, His children.

Learn for Yourself

It is so easy to rely on others to teach us the things of God. As young Christians we certainly need this. Jesus compared young Christians to little children. Little children need to be fed by older people, but as they grow up they start to feed themselves.

There are various ways we get fed by others .... all are good, and will continue throughout our lives, but we need to learn to feed ourselves too. Some of the common ways others feed us are:

- Listening to Sermons/Talks in Churches and Groups.
- Reading Christian books
- Listening to or watching Podcasts or YouTube videos of Christian teachers or discussions

These all help, and some authors are particularly good at bringing Bible truths into day-to-day situations BUT God wants to speak directly to YOU through His Word; because He has things to show you that no-one else has ever seen, and it is so much more of a blessing to hear straight from God's Word than second hand from someone else.

Yet God cannot speak to us if we do not spend time listening. Yes, God can speak directly to us, yes there are gifts of dreams, visions, prophecies and the like. However, God is full of wisdom and *does not speak to us in such ways unless and until we are listening to Him through His Word.* So, if you are not regularly reading the Bible and yet think you hear God giving you directions, be very careful. If it is not based on Bible knowledge it is likely not to be God you are hearing at all. Reflect on what others teach of the Bible, reflect on your own reading of it and you will find you are beginning to hear God speak to you more clearly.

You see, without knowing what He says in the Bible we have no plumb-line to measure whether what we think are 'words from God' are likely to be real or not, we will not know what we need to guard against. The Bible tells us to *be alert and of sober mind. Your enemy the devil prowls around like a roaring lion looking for someone to devour.* (1 Peter 5:8). If we know the Bible we can be clearer when we hear from God in other ways, and when it instead is our own imagination or even the Devil we are hearing.

There are four basic ways of reading and studying the Bible. ALL are important. In a sense they are like using different types of map:

  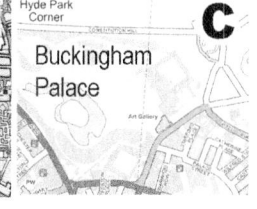

Map A gives a good overall picture; showing perhaps the main route: by road.	Map B shows lesser roads, and a smaller area in greater detail.	Map C shows everything about a small area, how the surroundings link together.
READING the Bible like any other book is like using this map: You get an idea of the main themes.	Its like *STUDYING* a particular theme or character to get a good understanding of it/them.	Slow, verse by verse, study of God's Word helps us to hear God clearly.

The fourth method of studying the Bible is *MEMORISING* it. Then it remains with you even when you are not carrying it around. Its not as difficult as you think, as a teenager I memorised most of the London Tube map just by using the Tube and looking at it 'for fun'. In the same way we memorise Bible verses by having favourite passages which we often read or perhaps by singing them if they're set to music. Much of the words which are used in the written parts of Church of England services are also straight from the Bible. You'll be surprised how many of these you know already (can you complete them from memory beyond what is written?):

> Matthew 6:33 *Seek ye first the Kingdom of God....*
> Philippians 4:4 *Rejoice in the Lord always...*
> Psalm 40 *I waited patiently for the Lord, He turned to me and heard my cry*
> John 3: 16 *God so loved the world that He gave....*
> Deuteronomy 31:6 *Be strong and courageous...*
> Matthew 7:7 *Ask and it will be given to you....*
> Isaiah 52:7 *How lovely on the mountains are the feet.....*
> Psalm 23 *The Lord is my shepherd.....*
> Matthew 4:4 *Man shall not live on bread alone...*
> 1 John 1:8-10 *If we say we have no sin....*
> Revelation 4:8 *Holy,holy, holy, is the Lord God Almighty....*
> Matthew 6:9-13 *Our Father in heaven, hallowed be Your Name...*

So it is important to give a good deal of time to reading the Bible and studying it. It is worth at this point mentioning our need to pray too. Make reading the Bible part of a conversation. Ask God to help you to be illuminated in some way by your reading and as you are ask Him to help you to remember what you read, change the way you do things, or simply pray that His Kingdom will come and His Will be done in accordance with what you have been reading.

Getting started

It does not matter how long you have been a Christian, you will probably be feeling a shade guilty about your Bible Study habits by now. We never get to the stage of being satisfied we are doing enough, but we should not get guilty over it. The Bible tells us that, as Christians, we are no longer under condemnation (Romans 8:1, read the whole chapter!). God does not condemn us, Satan does. And if he can keep us feeling miserable about it then we won't properly get into the Bible:

The same can be said for Prayer and Witnessing (telling others the Good News of Jesus) .... there's always more that can be done; its no use feeling bad about what we have not done, we need to get on and do what we can do.

So let's start by suggesting ways for each of the three maps above:

ONE: READING THE BIBLE

Obviously the easiest method to start; but you need a plan. It is clearly in your interest to get to know the whole Bible. It is good to know that there are certain themes which run all the way through it; such as Love, Redemption, Justice, and so on. Also it is good to see God's Master Plan: how He created everything to be Good, then our sin ruined it and we lost the opportunity to eat from the Tree of Life and live forever (Genesis 3); the rest of the Old Testament consists of God's faithfulness to His People despite their unfaithfulness and also of promises of a coming Messiah, getting louder and clearer as the time drew near.
The New Testament presents us with the Messiah Jesus, demonstrates the depth of God's love in His Plan for our Salvation; and concludes in Revelation with a classic story book ending: The Tree of Life, lost to humanity in Genesis is restored to us in Revelation 22; and we can live forever and it is all good again!

But more than that, each individual book. is also a book in its own right. Each one has its own beginning, its own message and its own definite ending. So you don't have to start at Genesis 1 and read straight through to Revelation 22. In fact, that isn't the way God intends us to read it. We live in the Age of the Church, and the clearest teachings for the Church arc found in the Gospels, Acts and the Epistles ... the New Testament.

So a good reading plan would be to start with the New Testament. There are no right ways and wrong ways of reading through the Bible, you will develop your own scheme as you continue to read. Sometimes you will just 'feel' like something from the Old Testament, other times you will hear a sermon from a book and want to read more. But I suggest the following as a rough guide to help:

First realise that you will only begin to understand the message of the Old Testament (which us largely given through the examples of how God dealt with Israel and other nations through history) when you understand the teachings in the New Testament which is largely verbal instruction.

A Plan for Reading

There are many ways of dividing the Bible up. One way is as follows:

  i] LAW: Genesis to Deuteronomy
  ii] HISTORY+POETRY: Joshua to Song of Solomon
  iii] PROPHETS: Isaiah to Malachi
  iv] GOSPELS: Matthew to John
  v] ACTS
  vi] LETTERS: Romans to Jude
  vii] REVELATION

I suggest you start to read with the Gospels, then you will be ready to look at the Law, come back to Acts, then History and so on. (A guide would be the order [iv] [i] [v] [ii] [vi] [iii] [vii].) But that does not have to be rigidly stuck too, and there arc other equally sensible routes through the Bible (you will find a more detailed plan for starting at the end of this book).

Perhaps a starting off scheme, loosely based on the above, would be:
1> MATTHEW, MARK or LUKE
2>JOHN
3> one of the other two GOSPELS

Having read three Gospels you now have a pretty good picture of what Jesus came to do; perhaps it is time to see what the problem was....
4> GENESIS

Now read about how the first of Jesus' followers carried the message in the early days of the Church
5> ACTS

6> the fourth GOSPEL
7> EPHESIANS
8> I JOHN to 3 JOHN
9> EXODUS
10> GALATIANS, PHILIPPIANS and COLOSSIANS
11> PSALMS

and so forth. LEAVE Revelation and Hebrews till you really know the Old Testament.

The History books of the Old Testament (up to Job) are easier to follow than the Prophetic ones (Isaiah onwards). Proverbs can be read often, verse by verse almost, as it is a book of wise sayings.

Remember, the History books record God's faithfulness to His People and you should read them with that in mind. The Prophetic books warn of the folly of not following God but always link it with the promise of His faithfulness and that all the 'troubles' are discipline not vengeance.

By reading in this sort of way you will get to know the Gospel message first, before you look at Creation and God's early dealings with us. The Law (Exodus to Deuteronomy) will then make much more sense. Even Leviticus will begin to speak as you realise through it how seriously God views sin ... which is what the book is all about really. Numbers could be left until much later, move on into the other history books first.

So read New Testament books most, and go back to the Old Testament every now and then. Gradually you will begin to hear God speaking dearly to you in the OT too ... a sure sign that your Bible reading habits arc bearing fruit.

Always spend time re-reading the Gospels. Perhaps every Christmas and Easter time choose one to read right through in a day or so. That way the main message of the Bible, the Person or Jesus, will always be in focus.

When you read a book you should aim to take no more than a week or perhaps two to read it all. None or the books of the Bible arc long compared to most paperbacks available today.

It is important to choose a translation (or version) of the Bible that you can read easily. There are 'scholarly' translations which try to get to the deepest meanings of the original Hebrew or Greek phrases being translated and there are also 'easy read' translations that aim to make the Bible accessible to all.

The good news is that you don't have to buy the translations in order to decide which is best for you, there are now Apps or online websites that have the whole Bible in a range of translations.

Finding the right translation

If you are an App-lover, download either or both of YouVersion or Bible Gateway. Alternatively, visit www.biblegateway.com on your desktop browser.

Whichever way you are doing it, you will see you can choose both a passage to read and a translation to read it in, and compare them. A good way is to choose a passage you know quite well and look at the way it is written in different versions (if your first language isn't English, you will also find a translation into your own language there as well)

Here's the first few verses of Psalm 23 in four different translations:

NEW INTERNATIONAL VERSION -UK
The Lord is my shepherd, I lack nothing.
He makes me lie down in green pastures,
he leads me beside quiet waters,
he refreshes my soul.
He guides me along the right paths
for his name's sake.
Even though I walk through the darkest valley,
I will fear no evil,
for you are with me;
your rod and your staff,
they comfort me.

GOOD NEWS TRANSLATION
The Lord is my shepherd;
I have everything I need.
He lets me rest in fields of green grass and leads me to quiet pools of fresh water.
He gives me new strength.
He guides me in the right paths, as he has promised.
Even if I go through the deepest darkness,
I will not be afraid, Lord,
for you are with me.
Your shepherd's rod and staff protect me.

EASY-TO-READ VERSION
The Lord is my shepherd.
I will always have everything I need.
He gives me green pastures to lie in.
He leads me by calm pools of water.
He restores my strength.
He leads me on right paths to show that he is good.
Even if I walk through a valley as dark as the grave,
I will not be afraid of any danger, because you are with me.
Your rod and staff comfort me.

YOUNG'S LITERAL TRANSLATION
Jehovah [is] my shepherd, I do not lack,
In pastures of tender grass He causeth me to lie down, By quiet waters He doth lead me.
My soul He refresheth, He leadeth me in paths of righteousness, For His name's sake,
Also ~ when I walk in a valley of death-shade, I fear no evil, for Thou [art] with me, Thy rod and Thy staff ~ they comfort me.

By the way, if you select New International Version - UK (NIVUK) there is an option for it to be read to you, and the reader is celebrated actor David Suchet.

For reading, choose a translation with easier English such as the Good News or Easy-to-Read but for study you need to use one or two of the weightier translations and compare them when they are different and think about the wording.

Whichever option you opt for though you should definitely get a printed version and be ready to use a pen in it to underline or highlight places where God speaks to you specially, it then becomes something of a life journal of your journey with God.

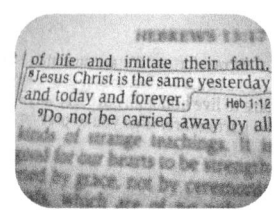

TWO: STUDYING THEMES OR CHARACTERS

When you have read a book it is helpful to begin to look at it more closely. One way to do this is to get a notebook and make a Chapter Summary. In your own words write down the main points of each chapter. In the Gospels there may be several (e.g. a parable, a miracle, some teaching etc). In a letter see if you can spot the main message of that letter. DON'T start to study a book until you have READ it!

But when you are ready for a deeper study, ask questions such as:

> What are the main points of this chapter?
>
> Is there an example here for me to take notice of? Is it a bad one (something to avoid?) or a good one (something to emulate?) etc.
>
> Is there a promise that I can lay hold of and pray about for myself, my family, my church, my nation?
>
> Is there a command that I need to obey?

Or you might choose a character and study their life. David is a good one, for instance, How did he follow God, what happened when he sinned, what sort of person was he, what does God want me to learn from his life? Remember David appears in more than one book (1 & 2 Samuel, Psalms, and several mentions in the New Testament) so there's lots to look up. There are many other characters, Noah, Ruth, Paul, Peter and so forth; each study could well take many months!

Again, write down what you think about. File the notes you make and read them through later on; either when you come to study or read the book again or at the end of every few months. That way you help yourself to remember what you learn.

You will begin to see that you need resources to help you.

As a minimum I would say you need a Bible which includes Cross References. Of course, the web versions and Apps contain all of this but some printed Bibles do and some do not. A cross-reference is a note which says which other verses are linked to the one you are reading either by being exactly the same or by following a similar theme.

Cross References are featured at the bottom of the page or, sometimes, down the central column. They link together other verses which speak of the same word or theme as the verse you are looking at. Bibles with these are often called 'Chain Reference' editions.

If you have some money to spare it would be helpful to buy a Commentary on the subject or character you are studying. There are normally several to choose from and Bible bookshops are well stocked. Look for one which seems easy to understand. Check to see if it includes background information (historical facts about the time it was written, fulfillments of prophecies contained in the book, etc). Perhaps ask your vicar/minister or other older Christians jf they have one you can borrow.

My advice is not to look at a Commentary (apart from getting an understand of geographical or historical background) until after you have studied the themes yourself, to fill in what you have missed out. Don't accept what it says necessarily. If you disagree fine; discuss it with someone else. You are as likely to be right as the author, for the Holy Spirit speaks to each of us, and will often reveal something to you about the passage that He hasn't done to the author of the commentary.

Many Bibles contain charts or maps. You should look at these too as they are a good way of learning about the places and customs of the day.

WARNING. Its very easy to rely on the commentary. Use it as a tool but remember IT is NOT Scripture. It is liable to follow the biases of the author which is of course something we all bring to our reading of Scripture. That's why a good part of study is to get together with other Christians to talk about the book you are studying and to see if from different perspectives. Studying the Bible like this with a friend is an excellent way of providing motivation. You can either work through it together or agree which book you will by studying alone and then get together regularly to compare notes and talk about it.

THREE: VERSE BY VERSE

Now we come to the slowest form of study; but also the most worthwhile. Again, you should not study a book like this unless you have (recently) read it through and know its main theme.

I read each verse as it comes and then write down in my own words what it means. I also write down other thoughts it sparks off, linking in other similar verses (cross-references again). If there are words I don't understand then I look them up in a dictionary or ask. If there is some teaching I don't understand then I ask someone.

The purpose of all this study is to get to know God and hear what He is saying to me. So I read asking questions such as:

> Is there a Promise here that I can claim for myself?
> Is there a Command here that I must obey?
> Is there an Example here that I should follow or should avoid?

I rarely manage to cope with more than 7 or 8 verses at a time like this (and that takes over half an hour!) so it is a slow process getting through a book. Yet as I study often there is a verse that is especially meaningful which I will write down or memorise. And rarely do I finish the time without knowing that God has been speaking to me.

Again, I file the notes for future reference. It would be a good habit to read through all the notes every time you finish a book. That way you review things you have done in the past and keep it all fresh in your mind.

Remember that the purpose of your study is found in 2 Timothy 3:16,17 It should be profitable to you and teach you, rebuke you where necessary and correct your thinking in order that you might become thoroughly equipped for every good work. Pray that what you learn may become lifestyle and not just head fact.

With that in mind you should always pray before you start to read the Bible. Not just a quick 'speak to me God' but Bible reading/study should be part of a real time of prayer WITH (not TO) God. In the same way your Bible reading/Study should lead you to pray.

How Long?

You should aim at about 15 minutes of reading every day (3-4 chapters, at this rate you could read the whole Bible in one year). Do it at a time when you know it will sink in.

Also, 2 or 3 times a week some Quick Study, perhaps aiming to keep up with the book you are reading and note down important points from it.

At least once a week a time of verse by verse study, working very slowly through a book.

But if all that seems too much DON'T WORRY! The important thing is that you read God's Word at all! Make a realistic plan for yourself. It may well be that Level 3 is too much for you, even Level 2. (Who said Level 1?!). It may be that 5 minutes a day; or even 20 minutes a week, is more than what you do at the moment and that is all you call plan for. OK - SO DO THAT! But remember ..... it is worth putting some effort and sacrifice into it. How much time do you waste in front of the TV?

It is important not to try to do the 'deeper' study until you want to, otherwise it may turn you off for life. So as you read pray that God will give you a greater hunger for His Word; then you will find yourself naturally going into it deeper.

TOOLS

I have not mentioned Bible Reading Notes. I feel that it is too easy to rely on what someone else has written. It is far better to learn for yourself. However, there are some tools you may decide you want as you go on, as your hunger demands more of God's Word in your life:

Study Bible Featuring explanatory notes, cross-references, maps, charts, ... and the Bible as well!
Commentary Either on a book or character or on the whole Bible
App or Website. You can search for a half-remembered verse, or other verses containing the same thoughts as the one you are reading
Bible Dictionary Explains terms, gives background on places and people from archaeology and historical writings. More of an encyclopaedia really. Again, no need to buy a physical book as you can find all this within the Apps/Websites.
Other translations Don't rely on just one, read several especially for study

And Finally .....

Remember the Bible is the Word of God. It is totally consistent with itself. All apparent contradictions are cleared up when you understand the situations referred to better. If in doubt ask someone and discuss it!

Life Changing

Be prepared for your pre-conceived ideas to change as you read the Bible.

How you understand the account of Creation and Adam and Eve is no doubt affected far more by TV, Science and commonly held views than by prayer and Bible reading. As you read the Bible such things will be brought into question. When this happens examine the problem prayerfully. There are a number of talks on YouTube by Christians who are scientists and who believe the Genesis account to be accurate, several are linked on this page (from my *12 Hours Course*): www.tinyurl.com/BibleBookVideos

That is not to say that there aren't different Christian approaches to the so-called tough bits. But what is important is that you examine the Bible under God's Light and not Human reason: *Trust in the Lord with all your heart and lean not on your understanding* Proverbs 3:5.

One of the common problems is that people think Paul was tough on women; and they are forbidden to teach in churches. 1 Timothy 2: 11,12 says *A woman should learn in quietness and full submission. I do not permit a woman to leach or have authority over a man.*

Now that seems clear enough. The problem is that Scripture is consistent, and in other places it says all are equal in God's sight. There is also the case of Priscilla, who we read of in Acts, and who was a Church leader approved of by Paul.

The background to all this is important. Jewish boys went to school and were taught the scriptures up to twelve years of age. Jewish girls stayed at home and were taught about housekeeping by their mothers until someone came to marry them. A popular Jewish prayer was *'ThankYou God that I was not born a woman!'*. In the synagogue the men gathered in one place to listen to the scriptures and the Rabbi. The women were separated and chatted to each other during the service, not considered able to understand it.

In the light of this, the verses above take on a new meaning. Now we read *why* women had to be silent: to listen to God's word just like the men. They cannot teach because they have not received an education in the scriptures.

There are other verses which relate to women becoming Priests which cause some to have problems, largely because the concept of 'Priest' as we understand it today is not found in the New Testament and is built on tradition, not Scripture, and there is not space to examine them all here. The point I am making is not about women Priests but about how we must understand the Bible in its original context and not to read 21st Century culture into the text.

So if you find a passage which does not make sense or is hard to understand it is good to ask or read about the background and to think for yourself and pray about it.

There are hard bits to understand but if you start from the idea that it all fits together you will get there in the end!

WHO WROTE THE BIBLE?

Some people argue about whether this bit or that bit was written by the same person as the rest of the book (e.g. did Moses write Genesis 1-11 or not?).

If you believe that the bible was inspired by the Holy Spirit, given as He wants it to be, then it does not matter who wrote it down. In many places there is no clue even to the name of the writer, what is important is that we read it and obey it.

The important question is not WHO WROTE IT but WHO READS IT?!!

Ways to Start

If you are someone who has not regularly read the Bible before, there is a suggested plan for the first month in the next few pages.

First, you need access to a Bible. You may well have one on your shelves somewhere but it is likely to be an Authorised (or King James) version. It was a good translation in its day but it is now full of words we no longer use and some which mean almost the opposite of what they originally did, so it is not recommended for a beginner. Use it alongside a modern translation by all means, but the aim of Bible study is not to have nice poetic language but to be able to hear what God is saying today.

If you want to buy a Bible and do not know of a local Christian Bookshop, I recommend Eden.co.uk which has a large range of Bibles, it is linked on the resource page for this book (see bottom of the page). Alternatively you can visit a Bible website such as Bible Gateway or use a Bible App (YouVersion for instance). These are also linked on our website resource page.

Once you have a printed Bible, do not be afraid to write in it, underline it, highlight it. It is your book in which God will speak to you and the more you annotate it the more you will see how He has spoken to you over the weeks, months and years.

Our time of praying and reading is a time of *conversation* with Almighty God. He wants to speak to us but He also wants to listen to us. The more time we give to this the more we will hear Him, but there will be a process of 'tuning in'. You might not 'hear' anything at first when you start to read. Hopefully, by the end of the first month you will be beginning to recognise how God speaks to you through His Word.

Visit our resource page at www.lumin.org.uk/BibleBook

START WITH A PRAYER

I am assuming for now that your time of Bible reading is a different time to your general praying, but you can of course combine the two.

Before you start to read the Bible you should ask the Holy Spirit, who is its Author, to open your heart and mind to hear what He has to say. You can make up your own prayers for this but here are a few you might choose to use which are based on Bible verses.

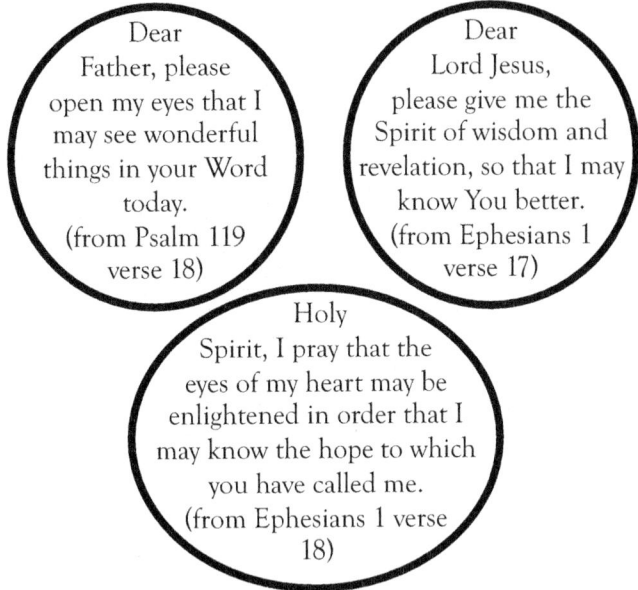

Dear Father, please open my eyes that I may see wonderful things in your Word today. (from Psalm 119 verse 18)

Dear Lord Jesus, please give me the Spirit of wisdom and revelation, so that I may know You better. (from Ephesians 1 verse 17)

Holy Spirit, I pray that the eyes of my heart may be enlightened in order that I may know the hope to which you have called me. (from Ephesians 1 verse 18)

ARE YOU SITTING COMFORTABLY?

You should be sitting comfortably, perhaps with a tea or coffee to hand and read through the passage you have for the day (read it aloud if you are alone, it helps you to concentrate on it).

Then think about what you have read for a minute or two and then re-read the passage more slowly. This time have a pen and notebook to hand, as you read make a note or two.

If there is something you don't understand, put a question mark on your notebook and write down the sentence or phrase you are not sure about.

If there is something that strikes you as being significant then underline it or highlight it *in your Bible* and also write it in the notebook, with a box around it or other marking to make it clear. If you are using YouVersion there is a way of highlighting the verse in different colours on the App. Here's a page of my Bible to show you how it gets added to over the years.

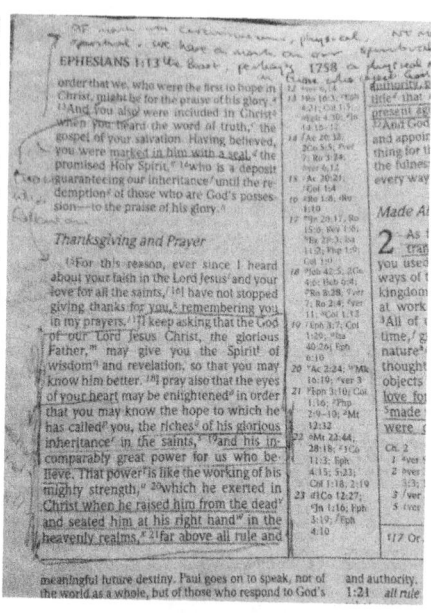

Now pray again, asking that God will help you with what you didn't understand and to remember what was significant.

'Significant' might mean it is something you had not realised before, it might be a promise that God gives to His people which you need to believe, or it might be a command or instruction which you feel you need to begin to obey.

Don't be afraid of going to a church leader or a friend who has been a Bible reader longer than you have to ask them about the bits you don't understand.

Suggested First Month Study Plan

I am going to suggest that you start with the Gospel of Luke and also some Psalms. The Gospel helps you to get to know what Jesus was like on earth and the Psalms are prayers or songs of praise from the days of King David and others. When you read about Jesus remember that the Bible says that He is truly God and His character reflects that of the Father. *The Son is the image of the invisible God, the firstborn over all creation. For in him all things were created: things in heaven and on earth, visible and invisible, whether thrones or powers or rulers or authorities; all things have been created through him and for him.* (Colossians 1 verses 15 and 16).

I will suggest five readings per week, giving you a couple of days to catch up if you miss a day (try not to!!). If you have completed the readings in five days then use the other two days to review, trying to remember what seemed important from each reading and also re-reading some of the passages.

Week One

1 Luke chapter 1 verses 1 to 25 (usually written as Luke 1:1-25)
2 Psalm 1
3 Luke 1:26-38
4 Psalm 2
5 Luke 1:39-56

You will notice there are different styles of writing, from narrative prose to poetic laments and others. You might find you prefer one type over another but one important way of understanding the Bible is to recognise the type of writing involved. You don't expect poetry to necessarily be literally true but to paint a picture of a deeper truth perhaps whilst on the other hand narrative is an account of actual events.

In your notebook write down the main thing you have understood, learnt or sense God has said to you from these readings this week.

Now let's continue with the rest of the month:

Week Two

1 Luke 1:57-80
2 Psalm 3
3 Luke 2:1-20
4 Psalm 4
5 Luke 2:21-40

Does the way the person praying in the Psalms speaks to God surprise you? What does it say about how we can pray?

Week Three

1 Luke 2:41-52
2 Psalm 5
3 Luke 3:1-23
4 Psalm 6
5 Luke 4:1-13 (we'll leave the end of chapter 3 for another time!)

Week Four

1 Luke 4:14-30
2 Psalm 7
3 Luke 4:31-44
4 Psalm 8
5 Luke 5:1-11

By now you should have established a pattern which you can develop in your own way. If you keep it up for another month you should have developed a habit which will last a lifetime!

Going Deeper

Deeper Bible Study involves getting to understand how the various books fit together, how some themes flow through the whole Bible and are developed and learning about the background to the passages in the text.

This takes time and is partly why I left the Bible reading to five days a week, if you can give more time at the weekend then that is the time for setting aside an hour for deeper study.

You could study a book, say one of Paul's letters such as Ephesians, or you could study a theme such as "Messiah" and see how that is developed through the Bible.

BibleProject My recommendation to help with this at least as a starting point is to visit The Bible Project online, which uses videos and podcasts to explore the Bible more deeply. The website is www.bibleproject.com and they also have a YouTube channel.

They have a great video that explains the Gospel of Luke and others for all the books of the Bible. A different set of videos explore the themes of scripture. It is all linked on the online resource page for this book.

The Bible Project is a launch pad for further study, at some point you will think "I want to know more about that" and that is the time to consider buying a book or two.

There is no right way to work through the Bible, you are beginning a conversation with the Holy Spirit and He will guide you in a journey that will bring fresh insights and revelation and help to shape you for the life you share with Him.

Have a great journey!

Visit our resource page at www.lumin.org.uk/BibleBook

How to Pray

Whilst this is not the subject of this book, perhaps you are now thinking about the way you approach God to pray.

Jesus taught His disciples that the way to approach God is to focus on Him first (*Our Father in heaven, hallowed be Your Name*) and then to align yourself with God's purposes (*Your Kingdom come, Your will be done on earth as in heaven*).

Only then do we start to focus on our own needs and wants (*Give us today our daily bread*) and begin to recognise our shortcomings (*Forgive us our sins as we also forgive others*).

Then we ask for his help and protection (*Do not lead us into temptation but deliver us from evil*) and finally we end by focusing on Him again (*For Yours is the Kingdom, the power and the glory, forever and ever*).

A mnemonic to help with this is A C T S:

<u>A</u>dore God, the Father, Son and Holy Spirit

<u>C</u>onfess to God what you are like, what you have done and be honest with Him

<u>T</u>hank Him for His goodness to you and the blessings of your life

<u>S</u>upplication - that means pray about 'Our Needs' - not just yours but those of family, friends, neighbours, your nation and the world.

The important thing is that it is a conversation with someone who reveals Himself to us as:
- Almighty God, King of kings - how would you speak to such an important person?
- Father - how do you approach a loving Father?
- Brother - how to you speak with a sibling?
- Bridegroom/Lover - how do you speak to a marriage partner?
- Saviour - how do you speak with the one who rescues you?
- ??? - as you read the Bible you will discover so many more ways that God reveals Himself to us. Use these discoveries to help you to approach Him in prayer.

Visit our resource page at www.lumin.org.uk/BibleBook

At different seasons of your life, often even at different moments of the day, you will want to approach Him in different ways. Use the ways they prayed in the Psalms to help you to develop your own relationship with Jesus.

I heard someone say recently that if you have a hobby, you get to know all about it. Your read magazines on it, you study it, you improve your skills, you are passionate when you talk to others about it.

As Christians, we should all *make the Bible our hobby*!

Printed in Great Britain
by Amazon